And
Miss Reardon
Drinks a Little

AND
Miss Reardon
Drinks a Little

by PAUL ZINDEL

RANDOM HOUSE   NEW YORK

TO *Betty,*

my remarkable sister, who

teaches me to survive

AND MISS REARDON DRINKS A LITTLE *was first presented on February 25, 1971, by James B. McKenzie, Spofford J. Beadle, Seth L. Schapiro, Kenneth Waissman and Maxine Fox, in association with Gordon Crowe, at the Morosco Theatre in New York City, with the following cast:*

(In order of appearance)

CATHERINE REARDON	Estelle Parsons
MRS. PENTRANO	Virginia Payne
DELIVERY BOY	Richard Niles
CEIL ADAMS	Nancy Marchand
ANNA REARDON	Julie Harris
FLEUR STEIN	Rae Allen
BOB STEIN	Bill Macy

Scenery by Fred Voelpel
Lighting by Martin Aronstein
Costumes by Sara Brook
Directed by Melvin Bernhardt

THE SCENE

The action takes place on an October evening, in the apartment of Catherine and Anna Reardon. The play is divided into three acts.

ACT ONE

The curtain rises on the comfortable apartment of CATH-ERINE *and* ANNA REARDON. *A visitor entering through the front door at stage left and surveying the apartment from left to right might notice the following: a desk and library area with various souvenirs from summer trips, a dining-room table near a swinging door to the offstage kitchen, a shadowed hallway leading to the bedrooms and the bathroom offstage, and finally a parlor into which it would seem no one had trespassed for many years.* CATHERINE REARDON *enters from the kitchen. She wears a simple blouse and skirt, and is carrying a tray of glasses and other items needed to mix drinks. As she puts the tray down on the desk and surveys the half-set dining-room table, the door buzzer sounds.*

CATHERINE (*Unlocking the front door and swinging it open to reveal* MRS. PENTRANO, *the wife of the superintendent of the apartment building in which* CATHERINE *and* ANNA *live*) What do you want?

MRS. PENTRANO Would you mind if I come in for a moment?

3

CATHERINE I'm sorry but I'm in a state of dishabille. Also, my bitch sister's coming for dinner.

MRS. PENTRANO *(Edging in)* My husband wanted me to check on the lock to make sure you're not having any trouble with it. He was blowing out the furnace but I told him the Reardons have always been nice to us, so he should go out of his way, especially the way Anna sounded so frightened on the phone. Does she like the lock?
(She closes the door)

CATHERINE She genuflected before it. Now, if you'll excuse me . . .

MRS. PENTRANO What I was wondering was, would you like to order some cosmetics? It's the holiday order, and most of the things you like are on sale.

CATHERINE I don't need anything, unless you've got bottled resurrection.

MRS. PENTRANO Oh, that's too bad because if I don't get my order in tonight, I'll lose the commission bonus. The Magno*l*ia skin-softener is on special.

CATHERINE Mag*n*olia, Mrs. Pentrano. Not Magno*l*ia. And I don't want any. I tried it once, and I got out of the bathtub feeling like I'd just swum the Hudson.
(CATHERINE *starts back toward the desk where she has put the tray.* MRS. PENTRANO *laughs shrilly*)

MRS. PENTRANO Miss Reardon, you always make me laugh. I wish I had your sense of humor. I really do. *(Having gained entrance, she now sets herself down. She takes a catalog and order pad out of the shoulder bag she is carrying)*

CATHERINE Would you mind keeping your cackle down? Anna is resting.

MRS. PENTRANO Oh, I'm sorry. I forgot she wasn't feeling good. Can I put you down for a box of lilac pellets? They're on special.

CATHERINE Where did you hear Anna wasn't feeling *good?*

MRS. PENTRANO Anna? Oh—You mentioned it a couple of days ago in the lobby. I hadn't seen her . . . and . . . the way she sounded so scared on the phone this morning . . .

CATHERINE Oh . . .

MRS. PENTRANO It's no wonder she's sick, with all those chemistry things she's teaching. And watching all those brats making test tubes of stinky gases and setting off hydrogen explosions and injecting rat embryos with dioxyneuki something-or-other.

CATHERINE Dioxyribonucleic acid. *(Repeats slowly)* Dioxyribonucleic acid.

MRS. PENTRANO   How about a room deodorant? Kiss of Heather? Tropical Night?

CATHERINE   Tropical Night—that's the one you gave me last time, and it smelled like Morning in Bayonne.

MRS. PENTRANO   Kiss of Heather. You'll like that. Anna always takes a jar of bath crystals. *(She notes that on her pad)* Mrs. Adams hasn't been here in such a long time, has she? She was one of my best customers. Of course, your lovely mother was, too. *(As* CATHERINE *goes into the kitchen* MRS. PENTRANO *raises her voice)* A lovely . . . *(She remembers* ANNA *is resting and lowers her voice)* . . . lady. Lovely. *(The door buzzer sounds)* I'll get it!
   (She opens the door to admit a DELIVERY BOY *burdened with groceries)*

DELIVERY BOY   Hello, Mrs. P. *(*CATHERINE *enters from the kitchen)* Hi, Miss Reardon. How're you doing?

CATHERINE   Shut up, please. Put the stuff on the table.

DELIVERY BOY   I ain't making any noise.

CATHERINE   Am not, not "ain't." Did Mr. Catobin remember to wrap the chop meat separately?

DELIVERY BOY   Chopped. It's *chopped* meat, not "chop meat."

CATHERINE Just answer the question.

MRS. PENTRANO You're probably due for body pow-
der.
(She jots down an order)

CATHERINE *(To the* DELIVERY BOY *as she takes a package out
of the grocery bag)* Is this it?

DELIVERY BOY I think so.

CATHERINE *(Taking the chopped meat out of the bag and
arranging it in an empty Fanny Farmer candy box)*
What do you mean you "think so"? If you don't start
being more precise, you're going to be nothing but
a delivery boy all your life. Do you know how un-
prepossessing it can be to be a sixty-four-year-old-
delivery boy?

MRS. PENTRANO The satchets . . . *(She pronounces it so
that it rhymes with "hatchets")* . . . are on special,
too.

CATHERINE *(Paying for the groceries)* Sachets, Mrs. Pentrano. Sachets, not *satchets.*

DELIVERY BOY Is your sister still sick, Miss Reardon?
I was in her Applied Chem class. That was one of
the classes she acted a little sick in.

CATHERINE Haven't I seen you down in the Dean's
Office recently?

7

DELIVERY BOY When Mr. Goodman threw me out of Personality Development for sneezing. He said I spit on him.

CATHERINE You have the face of a boy that would do gruesome things.

DELIVERY BOY Tell me, do you always put chopped meat in candy boxes? Some people might think that was gruesome.

CATHERINE All right, fat trap. You can get out of here.

MRS. PENTRANO You've got a fresh mouth on you, young man.

CATHERINE I'd tip you, but it's against my profession.

DELIVERY BOY You can say *that* again!
  (He darts out, leaving the door ajar)

CATHERINE *(Calls after him)* Don't be disrespectful to someone as dignified as I, or you'll end up with a pair of knuckles in your eyeballs! Mrs. Pentrano, you've got to beat it, too.

MRS. PENTRANO With kids like that in her class, it's no wonder Anna flipped.

CATHERINE I beg your pardon? Where did you hear that Anna . . . flipped?

MRS. PENTRANO Oh, I'm sorry. I didn't *mean* anything, I really didn't. I just heard . . . it was the kids
that got her a little . . . I mean . . . *(She moves toward
the door under* CATHERINE'*s glare)* The lock . . . I hope
she feels better with the new lock. With all those
things happening nowadays, I don't blame her.
Really, I don't blame her for . . . anything that's
happened to her. Those Lebonons fighting in the
alley last night scared half the neighborhood. It was
awful. Mrs. Greer in 4D called the police, but they
were gone by the time they got there. Anna always
gets an eye pencil.

CATHERINE *Lebonons? What Lebonons?*

MRS. PENTRANO Don't tell me you didn't hear those
two women punching each other like a couple of
prize fighters last night? They were screaming at the
top of their lungs in the alley. You didn't hear that?

CATHERINE Those were not Lebonons, Mrs. Pentrano. Those were *Lesbians.*
    (CEIL ADAMS *appears in the doorway. Her presence is
    imposing. She carries a brief case.* MRS. PENTRANO *sees
    her and is somewhat apprehensive at the sight of her)*

MRS. PENTRANO Hello, Mrs. Adams.

CEIL Hello, Mrs. Pentrano.

MRS. PENTRANO *(Awkwardly)* Welcome home.

CEIL   Thank you, Mrs. Pentrano.

(By the tone of her voice, CEIL *dismisses* MRS. PEN-
TRANO, *who then slips by her and exits into the hall,
closing the door after her)*

CATHERINE   Well, well, well. I never thought you'd
show up. Of course, that's not quite true.

CEIL   I had asked to come.

CATHERINE   Oh, sure, but it wouldn't be the first time
your busy, busy schedule would cancel out a lovely
family dinner. What do they have you supervising
down there at the Board of Ed? The Christmas
party? It's October, so I guess they're starting to
make the tree decorations.

CEIL   I had intended to call before this.

CATHERINE   Oh yes, I'm sure. Superintended. Do you
realize you haven't been here to see us since we put
Mother in her grave? A couple of lousy phone calls
in seven months, you little bitch.

CEIL   *(After a suitable pause)*   Where's Anna?

CATHERINE   She's "sedated." Do you want a Manhattan?

CEIL   Yes, please. She hasn't been teaching since last
Thursday?

CATHERINE Oh, cut the crap, Ceil.

CEIL Look, I wouldn't be here now if Hamilton didn't call and . . .

CATHERINE Sister, that tone of voice of yours butchers me, dear.

CEIL He suggested . . .

CATHERINE Sibling, sweets, your penultimate shortcoming has become the fact that you've taken so many graduate education courses you've ended up with euphemism of the brain. Nobody does anything at that Board without checking with you first —the overdressed Sheena of the Blackboard Jungle.

CEIL Jesus Christ, you forget!

CATHERINE Forget! Nobody forgets! Every teacher in that demented little school looks at me and silently burps in my face every day of the week. Where would you be if it wasn't for that powerhouse of a sister of yours? Know what the faculty has nicknamed you this year? Well, it's "superman." You have finally transcended womanhood entirely.

CEIL Catherine, what's the matter with Anna?

CATHERINE Matter? Who says there's anything the *matter?* Just because she started crying now and then—like right in front of her classes? I don't know where you got the idea something was the matter. Well, maybe she just wanted a little change of routine, like Mrs. Miniken at Oakwood High. Remember Mrs. Miniken? Mrs. Miniken, who leaped from the school roof and splattered herself all over the handball courts. Now, that was a change of routine. Mrs. Miniken—splat—all because of some marital difficulties, wasn't it? And she taught Family Living.

CEIL She hasn't been the same since Mama died, has she?

CATHERINE Now look, Ceil. We might as well be honest about this whole thing. The only thing you're disquieted about is how much nuisance Anna is going to cause you. How much trouble. How much mortification. How much money. I mean, let's face it. That's what's got you out of your condominium, isn't it?

CEIL Actually, Catherine, the only unkind remarks I've heard lately have been about you.

CATHERINE Oh, is that so? Well, I'm not interested. In fact, you may not even have to worry much longer about my nepotistically endowed assistant principalship, because I'm thinking of quitting and becoming a waitress. I could do with a little honest work for a change.

CEIL They say you've started to drink a little.

CATHERINE *(Stirring a huge pitcherful of Manhattans with a ruler)* What a preposterous and cruel disestimation. Who would hoot such a thing about me? Could it be one of your old friends from around here? One of our mutual friends before your nuptials? Was it Mr. Pollack in Apartment 2A, who beats his wife because she's having sex with the Fuller Brush man? Or was it Mrs. Pedowicz in 4C, who beats her husband because he's having sex with the Fuller Brush man?

CEIL It doesn't matter who said it.

CATHERINE What do you mean, it doesn't matter? They've got *one hell* of a nerve.

CEIL Actually, it was someone from your own school.

CATHERINE Someone from that bibliophilic looney bin? Who? Mrs. Drisser, that pygmyess with the face like Toto, the kissless bride? Or Lipschitz, who wears the same suit for six months and putts around with Gorgonzola of the breath? That whole pack of academically defunct, eternally matriculated and fuckingly overpaid nuts and what are they saying? Miss Reardon drinks a little. Jesus Christ!
(She pours two Manhattans)

CEIL   Look, if you've already had too much, I'll come back in the morning.

CATHERINE   No! *(A pause)* Well, maybe it was Mama's death that got her. And maybe it wasn't. I thought she got over that nicely, considering . . . Don't you, Ceil?
(She takes the candy box and nibbles at its contents intermittently)

CEIL   Was she all right on the trip?

CATHERINE   Oh, she did fine, just fine, till we got to Rome, that is; then she picked up this flea-bitten, ugly cat. There she was, running around the whole city picking up cats: black ones, green ones, yellow ones, three-legged ones, one-eyed ones—picking up any mangy sad thing she could get her hands on, while I was trying to get picked up by some of those two-legged smooth Italian tomcats—oh, I'm sorry, Ceil. I must sound crude to a happily married woman like yourself. Happily nuptialed to a big handsome man like Edward. How's Edward? Does he ask about me? *(A pause)* Oh, we mustn't go into that—must not we? Anyway, the night before we were going to leave for Naples for the tourist barge back, I finally found the Trevi Fountain and I was tossing my eighty-third coin, when Anna found this huge white cat, a tortured-looking thing, with a face like Goya's "St. Sebastian"—

CEIL El Greco's . . .

CATHERINE *Somebody's* St. Sebastian—and she picked it up, saying right into that hairy, festooned face, "Nice little pussy, pussykin. Nice little pussy, pussy." And the dear little thing responded by burying its front fangs into Anna's wrist. Right down to the bone.
(She takes a huge mouthful of chopped meat)

CEIL What the hell are you eating? Chop meat? *Raw* chop meat?

CATHERINE It's *chopped* meat, not chop meat. Fanny Farmer Chopped Meat.

CEIL Are you crazy? What on earth for?

CATHERINE Hold your water—you're rushing the story. So anyway, we laughed the cat bite off and go to Naples for this *Christoforo* trawler to get back here in time for school, which was to begin on September something or other.

CEIL School started September sixteenth.

CATHERINE Yes, Ceil, you're utterly correct. Utterly precise as usual. September sixteenth. And the afternoon before we docked, around September third—

try to pardon me for this temporal equivocation—docked in New York, Anna took an afternoon nap and had a nightmare—an afternoon-mare, if you will—and that evening she fainted in the dining room. To tell the truth, I was ready to pass out myself from the table-mates we got stuck with. I knew I should have tipped the maître d' on the gang-plank—this whole table of stag matrons who were so desperate they were sprinting after the busboys like piranha in evening gowns.

CEIL   Why did Anna faint?

CATHERINE   Well, Anna came to the conclusion she had rabies. But the ship's doctor told her not to worry, because if her symptoms were those of rabies she'd be dead in three days—which was sort of a fun prognosis. But three days later we were back here, and she was still having nightmares about some pregnant guppy or something, and we ran from doctor to doctor, each of whom told her not to take the antirabies injections because they were dangerous, and anyway the odds were one in a million that she had it. But she insisted on the shots, so for fourteen days we went to this senile quack down at the Board of Health and he stuck fourteen needles in her stomach, right *here*—pow, pow, pow!

CEIL   My God, how painful.

CATHERINE   On the contrary, Anna delighted in them. She looked like Somebody's St. Sebastian *smiling*.

CEIL   Then she was all right?

CATHERINE   No, she got worse. So I took her to a private senile quack and he put her on tranquilizers so she could get back to school, back to the beloved classroom, and he said everything she was bellyaching about was in her head. Anyway, I thought Anna was all right then or I wouldn't have let her go back to work. So she began once more to face the cheerful loving children. But they began to stalk her.

CEIL   What do you mean *stalk* her?

CATHERINE   In class. First they did the spitball routine —wang! Then the airplanes—zooooom! And the cow sounds—mooooo! mooooo! And the big thing last week, they were pinning flowers to her skirt without her knowing it and Scotch-taping little notes on her back like ONE OF MY TITS IS RUBBER and PLEASE MOUNT ME. Do you have any idea how embarrassing it can be to be the assistant principal of a high school and have your own sister arrive at the faculty conferences wearing a ONE OF MY TITS IS RUBBER sign on her back? It got so I had to check her clothes every period.

CEIL   Why do you think they began to do . . . dirty things to her?

CATHERINE Well, Jesus Christ, you've got us teaching condoms in kindergarten; positions in the third grade; abortion in the sixth; perverts, nymphos, satyrs and succubi in the eighth—if you ask me it's a wonder our kids aren't balling in the aisles.

CEIL Did Anna do anything to encourage the things they did?

CATHERINE I think she wore lipstick.

CEIL Catherine—the boy . . .

CATHERINE Oh, the boy! I was wondering how long it was going to take you to get to that. The cherub.

CEIL She sent for him.

CATHERINE The succulent seraphim who was present when Anna broke down—the McCloud boy . . .

CEIL He's saying—

CATHERINE You want to know about that little shit, I'll tell you. The nicest biographical detail on his grammar school record was that in the third grade he was caught pissing in a doll. During his first year in junior high he's taken dope, sold porno, and drew pictures of rhinoceri fornicating on the cover of his world geography textbook. Granted, he quieted down this term. He only punched a truant officer in the gut and just winks a lot as he walks around with his fly open. One of the semiliterate teachers in the English department dubbed him the Intermedable Tumescence.

(She takes a big mouthful of meat)

CEIL Would you stop eating that?

CATHERINE No. If I don't get some protein into me before Anna unsedates herself, I'm going to collapse.

CEIL What the hell does Anna have to do with your eating that disgusting raw meat?

CATHERINE Well, it's like this—ever since she broke down we're not allowed to eat flesh. You see, she's caressed vegetarianism. She made me throw out every piece of meat we had in the house. Even the bouillon cubes.

CEIL You're joking.

CATHERINE Yeah, I'm joking, but you'd better like zucchini, because that's what you're getting for supper. Saturday we had sautéed zucchini, Sunday we had boiled zucchini, Monday night for variety we called it squash. I can't even cook a codfish cake— "You've got no right to kill anything," she says. Monday night she rescued a cockroach out of the toilet bowl. It isn't bad enough we're paying over two hundred bucks a month for a co-op with cockroaches, I have to have a sister who acts as a lifeguard for them.

CEIL She's afraid of death . . . Maybe the way Mama died . . .

CATHERINE Oh, for Christ's sake, she's always been like that and you know it. Remember when Mama took us to St. Mary's Bazaar and we put her on that little Ferris wheel? There was only enough money for one, and Mama said she could go alone . . . remember?

CEIL Yes.

CATHERINE Jesus, I'll never forget her face when that motor started and she went up and up and up . . . (ANNA *suddenly appears in the hallway from the bedroom. She is wearing a bathrobe, and her hair falls loose about her shoulders*)

ANNA And I told them to stop—stop the machine.

CEIL Anna . . .

ANNA Oh, Ceil, I didn't know you were coming.

CATHERINE I told you nineteen times she was coming.

ANNA I forgot. I must have forgotten. I'm so doped up on tranquilizers and all those capsules. *(A pause)* I'm sorry, Ceil . . . I'm so ashamed, so ashamed.

(She sinks slowly, crying and puts her head on CEIL*'s lap)*

CATHERINE If you'll excuse me, I'll get dinner ready. I'm unsure of just how to peel a marinated zucchini. *(She goes into the kitchen)*

CEIL Anna, stop crying. I want to talk to you.

ANNA What did you come here for? She didn't even tell me you were coming.

CEIL I was concerned about . . .

ANNA Oh, my God—what a disgrace I've been to you, breaking down the way I did. I just couldn't give it back any more to all those snots.

CEIL Anna—get a hold of yourself.

ANNA *(Calling toward the kitchen)* Catherine! Did you ask her about the gun? Catherine, get back in here!

CEIL What gun?

CATHERINE *(Entering from the kitchen, peeling a squash)* I'll ask her now, and then you write it down so that tomorrow and all next week you don't keep asking me if I asked her. Ceil, when Mother died and you ramshackled this place for every piece of worthwhile silver, linen and glassware you could lay your hands on, did you also suck up Mother's pistol? Because if you *did* suck up Mother's pistol I wish you'd give it back so I can melt it down in front of Anna so she stops driving me crazy!

(*She exits into the kitchen*)

CEIL   That old gun Mama used to keep in the phonograph?

ANNA   Yes. The one that would have frightened burglars and mashers away if we had ever gotten any.

CEIL   (*Yelling toward the kitchen*)   Catherine! I resent the way you said that. I didn't ramshackle or suck up anything. I took a few of Mother's things just to save them. I just wanted to save them!

CATHERINE   (*Peeking her head in through the swinging door*) Bullshit!

(*She pops out of sight again*)

ANNA   Well, did you take the gun or didn't you, because I don't want it in this house!

CEIL   (*Yelling to* CATHERINE)   You still have that same filthy mouth!

ANNA   Why can't you admit whether you have it or not?

CEIL   I don't have it!

ANNA   Then it's here. I knew it was still here, and I'm afraid to have it in this house.
(She frantically begins looking for the gun)

CEIL   Anna, the gun only had blanks in it.

ANNA   Blanks? That's all it had in it, but couldn't someone have gone right down the street to Morrison's Sport Shop and bought some real bullets for it? It could kill someone right this minute, so I don't want it around—can't you get that through your skull?

CEIL   But nobody did buy real bullets for it.

ANNA   *(Searching through a desk and looking behind books in a bookcase)*   You tell me you know for sure someone didn't buy size 22 bullets for that gun—it could take size 22 real bullets, you know—you tell me you know for sure that right this minute that gun isn't in this house loaded and ready to kill and I'll call you a goddam liar!
(She throws a couple of books on the floor)

CEIL   What the hell are you afraid of?

ANNA   What am I afraid of?

CATHERINE   *(Entering with a pineapple on a plate, which she sets as a centerpiece)*   We were going to have carrot and beet juice for the appetizer because they're sup-

posed to be good for acne, boils and carbuncles—but I assume none of us have acne, boils, and carbuncles, so I thought crushed pineapple would be better.
(She goes back into the kitchen)

ANNA *(Continuing, to* CEIL*)* I'm afraid of someone putting a bullet into my brain, that's what I'm afraid of.
(She throws another book)

CEIL Stop throwing those books, please.

ANNA And last week, just before I became officially debilitated, we were discussing death in the 105 honors class—the one with all the brains—and I had them write all the ways of dying they could think of on the blackboards: fire, diphtheria, python constrictions, plane crashes, scurvy, decapitation—one kid remembered a little girl at Coney Island being run down by a miniature locomotive and getting a miniature death, and somebody else's uncle fell into a cement mixer in the Bronx and ended up as part of a bridge. By the end of the period we had the blackboards covered, crammed full of things— someone even thought of elephantiasis; we listed napalm and the bomb, and in the few seconds left to the class we all just sat back and wondered how the hell there were enough of us left alive to make up a class!
(She throws another book down, then retrieves it)

CEIL Stop it, Anna! *(A pause)* Why did you save that one?

ANNA It's Mother's Bible. She used to read it by proxy, remember? She'd have me read it when she was—atrophying—
(Her voice breaks)

CEIL Anna, I came here tonight—I want you to know it's taken me a while to get used to Mama's being gone, too.

ANNA That's very comforting of you, Ceil. Very comforting. But you've got a husband, and that helped you in your grief, I'm sure. I'll bet he's a pain in the ass, though. You must have loved him very much, Ceil—Havre de Grace, Maryland, wasn't it? Havre de Grace! Catherine and I would have loved to have come down for the wedding, but I guess it was simply too precipitous. I know what it must have been like being swept away by Edward's impetuosity.
(There is a pause)

CEIL Look, Anna . . .

ANNA Ceil, dear, you didn't get stuck with Mama like I did—watching her dehydrate, bounce up and down while her throat was closing. Did Edward remind you of our father? You know, I can't even remember what Papa looked like. I mean, I know his face from pictures in the albums—did you suck those up, too?

CEIL I didn't suck up anything!

ANNA *(Opening an album)* Oh, here it is. I mean, I was only three years old when he ran off to live with that skinny ostrich lady in Greenwich Village—123 Minetta Lane—but you and Catherine were nine, ten, remember? I couldn't go on the bus to see him at Christmas, but you two could . . .

CEIL *(Looking at a page in the album)* I remember . . .

ANNA Christmas. That was the only time you got to see him. All Mama would let me do was go along down to the bus stop, and then you and Catherine would go and get all the gifts and money you could grab; and Mama told you to smile at him, smile at your father, smile big, because then he'd give you more money and bigger dolls—and then she'd whisper sweetly, "Remember, girls, don't miss the bus back, and don't go with him if he tries to take you anywhere, and don't let him touch you between your legs, and then after you've finished smiling and after you've grubbed everything you can get, get right back on the bus and all the way home remember what a bastard your father is because he ran away with a skinny ostrich woman from Greenwich Village!"

CEIL *(Crying, from a memory)*   Oh, Mama . . .

ANNA *(Checking to see what picture* CEIL *is looking at)*   Oh,
I think her nose is too big in that one. *(She takes the
album and turns to the last page)* I like this one. I took
it three days before she died, with a 3.5 lens opening
and Tri-X film. I never thought it would come out,
there was so little light in the bedroom. She wanted
me to tell her about the Visions of the Apocalypse
that day, and I figured by taking her picture I could
make her forget, because I was ruining my eyes
from the little Biblical print. You need teensie eyes
for that sort of thing. You know, if I hadn't bought
The Holy Bible in Brief—that pocket edition put out
by Mentor Books—*Mentor!* I swear to God words
are weird!—if I hadn't bought it I would have gone
blind. So I told her about this one vision with the
horses—white, red, black and pale horses coming
out of the seals—CEIL!—the first four seals, *Ceil,*
and I got tired of reading so I told her the end of
Pinocchio. She liked that better than the horses. I
don't even know what a pale horse is.

CEIL *(Viewing the pathetic state of her sister)*   Oh, my
God . . .

ANNA   I'd cry too . . . but I don't think about it. I just
can't make sense out of anything any more. I
feel like I'm being wrapped in cellophane, my

mind . . . as though it's being coated with something and I can't help myself.

(CATHERINE *enters with a shaker of sunflower seeds, which she sprinkles on the pineapple appetizers*)

CATHERINE   Anna says these sunflower seeds are marvelous for vitamin C and roughage—but they knock hell out of your molars. (*To* ANNA) Did you tell sweetsie Ceil all about Rome and the cute little puddy-cat?

ANNA   (*Putting the album down*)   Do you think Mama was afraid of the world?

CATHERINE   One could suspect that a woman who kept a pistol in her phonograph and who locked the door even when her children went to put the garbage out was somewhat apprehensive.

(*She goes back into the kitchen*)

CEIL   Anna, what was the nightmare you had on the ship?

ANNA   Oh, that thing. It started with an aquarium filled with water—dripping with water—and I was standing outside, watching a guppy give birth to a whole batch of babies; and then the mother started devouring the little fish right as soon as they came out—but somehow she was the one who ended up disemboweled.

CATHERINE *(Entering)* Here's the zucchini, girls. Come and get it!

CEIL What a terrible nightmare.

CATHERINE If you wanted something else you should've brought it.

CEIL I was talking to Anna.

CATHERINE Did she tell you the part in the dream where she's running perpendicular along a beach?

ANNA *(As she sits down at the table)* There was water all around me and I hated the water. I was afraid of the water. In the dream . . .

CATHERINE That's right, Anna, you in the middle —and we'll put our lovely sister near the squash pot.

CEIL I'm not very hungry.

CATHERINE You're not hungry now, eh? Wait'll you get a mouthful of that crap.
(She hides the candy box of chopped meat on the seat next to her and sneaks from it during the meal)

CEIL Why do you think you fainted in the dining room, Anna?

CATHERINE First she's gotta tell you the little game the piranha in evening gowns were playing at the table when the hirsute busboys were in the kitchen. It was called: "Who Am I? Who Am I?" God, these sunflower seeds are tasty. Anna had told them about her encounter with the pernicious pussy cat at the Trevi Fountain, so this one desperate ruminating piranha, who wore dresses so low she looked like she was incessantly passing flesh-colored Idaho potatoes —this desperate forty-eight-inch-boobed piranha did a little pantomime which went like this *(With weird voice):* "Who Am I? Who am I?"

(She mimes picking up a cat, snuggling it in her arms, and then getting viciously bitten on the wrist)

ANNA Don't say any more, Catherine—please.

CATHERINE And so, Anna, with that babbling brook mouth of hers, insists on telling about her little dream—telling that whole table of bejeweled unrequited nymphos about all that water . . .

ANNA Please, Catherine . . .

CATHERINE And the pregnant guppy. Water, water everywhere, and how afraid she'd been of the water, so terrified of the water in her dream. And I'm sitting there trying to digest a poached perch while she's raving on about disemboweled guppies and that goddam water—a chemistry teacher afraid of H_2O—just absolutely terrified of water, when the piranha with the titanicly tuberous boobs says one word—one word—and Anna passed out right at the table.

CEIL What did she say?

CATHERINE Hydrophobia!

ANNA I fainted because I knew I had rabies. Hydrophobia—the *fear of water*—that's the first symptom of rabies in a human being. Animals don't get that symptom, but I had that warning in my dream . . .

CEIL Anna, if you had had any symptoms of rabies you would have been dead in three days.

ANNA *(Still eating, but her voice getting angry)* I'm quite certain I had rabies.

CEIL Anna, the doctors . . .

ANNA *(Screaming)* TO HELL WITH THE DOCTORS! *(Quieter)* They don't know anything about rabies, and one day they're going to find out that the first stage of rabies is not the one they think it is— that *vision* before you die. They're going to find out the first symptoms of rabies are dreams, dreams of doom before it's too late to get the shots, those horrible, horrible shots in the stomach!

CEIL *(Taking a mouthful of food—fighting against getting furious at* ANNA's *tone of voice)* Catherine told me you loved them.

ANNA   Yeah, but they were *supposed* to be horrible. I loved them because I needed them.

CATHERINE   What vision before you die?

ANNA   Those quacks think the first symptom of rabies is this vision—this vision when you're wide awake. The Vision of Doom, they call it. Three days before you die. Some day they're going to find out that the first symptom is a dream of doom, not a vision of doom. A dream when there's still time to do something about it.

CEIL   You didn't have rabies, Anna.

ANNA   I had rabies, YOU GODDAM STUPID FOOL!
   (CEIL *moves quickly away from the table*)

CATHERINE   (*Coughing gently*)   I think there's a jot too much pepper in the zucchini.

CEIL   Anna, we've worked very hard to get where we are. I fought for everything I've got . . . we've got. You're hurting all of us, Anna. (*Pauses*) I understand what you're going through. (*Pauses*) You had to take care of Mama . . . You had to clean her, hear her pain.

ANNA   What are you doing here now, Ceil? What are you doing in this friggin' room?

CEIL   The boy, Anna . . . the boy . . . you need love . . .

ANNA   Yes, but Catherine doesn't have any more studs to steal. Ceil, does it ever gnaw at that cybernetic soul of yours that Catherine's turned into the old maid you should have been? Take a good look at her. Catherine, how can you sit at the same table with the bitch that stole the only man that ever even liked you?

CATHERINE   Don't say any more, Anna . . .

ANNA   When she was still living here and Edward came to see you, couldn't you smell what she was doing? Her voice daintier than usual, an extra twinkle in her eye. She'd behave herself while you were in the room, but if you went out she always had a witty remark ready—some humoresque about her pension or salary, how she really needed help in managing her great big salary. *(She pauses)* And you got him, didn't you, Ceil, dear? *(She stands up)* Even if he was a schnook. He only married you because you had more loot . . . *(Sweetly)* . . . and you deserve each other, that *lying* titmouse and his superman. *(She pauses)* I need love? Tell us, Ceil, in this marriage—this regeneration of yourself in marriage—in that great distance you've traveled from Mama's table, why is it I'm looking into your eyes and still see a cripple?

CEIL Anna, we're going to have to do something with you.

ANNA No, Ceil—we're going to have to do something with you!
(She pulls a pistol from her bathrobe pocket and fires it three times, CEIL *practically collapses.* ANNA *waves a napkin to clear the air, resumes her place at the table and tucks her napkin under her chin very properly)*

CATHERINE *(She sips her drink, then says quite calmly)* Well, that was very nice, Anna. *(She takes the gun)* We'll just put the gun in the album, see? Right in the album, and then Ceil can just take the album and the gun with her when she goes. She'll take the gun, and then you won't have to be so timorous about it's being in the house. Ceil can just *save* them.

ANNA *(Sweetly)* Someone *could* have put real bullets in it.

CATHERINE *(Lifting her Manhattan glass in the gesture of a toast, then drinking)* That noise might have been just what we needed. Nowadays you need nice noises every so often—like Lebonons Indian-wrestling under your window.

Curtain

ACT TWO

PART TWO

The curtain rises. CATHERINE *finishes a sip of her drink and lowers the glass.*

CATHERINE   I think tonight we'll prepare the dessert at the table. It's got to be seen to be believed.
(She goes into the kitchen)

ANNA *(Calling to* CATHERINE*)*   Don't forget the kiwi fruit! *(She takes a big mouthful of zucchini, then addresses* CEIL*)* I really don't know who you think you are, coming in here believing you're going to do and say whatever you want, like a Queen Rhesus Monkey. Catherine and I pay the rent on this apartment now, so you're only a visitor, Ceil. A guest in the house, no longer the Queen Rhesus Monkey.
(She uses a pepper grinder on her food)

CEIL   The boy's family is going to . . .

ANNA   I DON'T WANT TO HEAR YOUR CRAP!

CATHERINE *(Entering with a large electric blender, which she sets on a sideboard and plugs in)*   Dessert is going to be a culinary treat your taste buds will never forget.

ANNA You have the kiwi fruit?

CATHERINE Yes, we have the kiwi fruit. Kiwis and kumquats. Kiwis and kumquats.
(She exits)

ANNA Ceil, your trouble is that you eat meat. That's why you have this hallucinatory problem—this conviction that you're a Queen Rhesus Monkey. Can't you feel what meat does to you—that slightly sickening feeling in your stomach after you've stuffed yourself with centrosomes? The kind of thoughts you have, the nightmares, warning you—aren't you aware of those things? Ceil, if you wanted roast pork could you just grab an ax and lop off a pig's head? Don't you see any connection between being able to slaughter an animal and killing a human being? You barbarian.

CATHERINE *(Entering with half a watermelon on a platter. She sets it down and proceeds to scoop out little balls, which she places in the blender)* When prepared and served artfully and with imagination, a vegetarian diet can be a gastronomic delight.

ANNA I didn't mean to scare you, Ceil. I love you, honest.

CEIL If there was a real bullet in that gun you would've used it just the same.

ANNA But no one did go out and buy real bullets. What are you so afraid of?

CEIL You would've killed me.

ANNA But I love you, Ceil. My own little sister. Don't you remember all the love between us, you and Catherine and me and Mama? All four of us! All that love. Oh, come on, Ceil, smile. Please smile. *(She goes to tickle* CEIL *under the chin)* Kitchykitchykoo!
(The door buzzer sounds)

CEIL Don't answer it.

ANNA You shut the hell up.

CATHERINE *(Heading for the door)* Yes, it might be one of your old friends.

CEIL Get rid of whoever that is.
(CEIL, *very much upset, goes off down the hallway to the bathroom.* CATHERINE *opens the door)*

CATHERINE Oh, Fleur.
(FLEUR *is wearing a voluminous fur stole, with a pants suit and an excess of costume jewelry)*

FLEUR Catherine, I tried to call you but the circuits were busy. We've missed you down at school. Really, we have. I mean, what good is a color-coordinated phone if you can't use the thing? Anna, darling . . . *(She promenades across to* ANNA*)* You poor thing. We've missed you dreadfully. How are you feeling?

(She goes to hug her)

ANNA *(Jerking away from the oncoming fur)* Get that away from me. Get it away.

FLEUR *(Unable to comprehend)* I'm sorry. I . . .

CATHERINE She doesn't like fur, Fleur.

FLEUR I'm terribly sorry. I didn't know that. I'll just take it off, then.

CATHERINE Let me hang it up for you.

FLEUR *(Putting it down)* Right here on the chair is fine.

CATHERINE You certainly pulled out all the stops to-night, didn't you?

FLEUR Oh, thank you. Bob and I are going to the theater, but I did allow some time to visit with you folks. I suppose you might say I'm on official business as the representative of the teachers' Social Committee, but Mrs. Pentrano stopped up at the apartment and told me Mrs. Adams was here—I did want to meet her. Bob's gone down to the car to get a little gift for Anna that the committee allotted the money for. I bought it this afternoon when Bob and

I were out shopping, but we left it in the car. *(Fur-less)* Now can I give my little Anna a hug?
>*(She promenades back to* ANNA *and gives her a short embrace)*

ANNA   What did you get me?

FLEUR   Gifts are supposed to be surprises, Anna. It's not very much, but it's a way to know that the faculty thinks of you when you're . . . ill. I was very limited in the amount of money the committee made available . . .

CATHERINE   Can I make you a drink?

FLEUR   I'm sorry but I don't drink. I gave up smoking in June. *(To* ANNA*)* My, what are you eating?

ANNA   Zucchini.

FLEUR *(Taking a saucer and a fork)*   I will try a little of this, if you don't mind.

CATHERINE   If you didn't eat, let me fix you a plate.

FLEUR   This is just fine. I just want to nibble. *(She begins to eat zucchini)* As I was saying, I was very limited in the amount of money the Social Committee made available. As you know, it's twenty-five cents a day if you're out on at least four consecutive days—Catherine, you weren't out four consecutive days, so nothing accumulated to get you a gift, though you are getting a card in the mail. But Anna was out four days in a row, which gave me only one dollar to work with ordinarily, but the committee is allowed to grant up to ten dollars if it looks like the teacher's going to be really sick, so you got the full ten dollars.

CATHERINE It's nice that it's so exact.

FLEUR I know it's ridiculously complicated but it's the only way to be fair. *Is* Mrs. Adams here?

CATHERINE She's in the john. I know she'd be happy if you could stay a while and meet her. She'd feel badly if you just dashed off.

FLEUR What *are* you making?

CATHERINE Dessert.

FLEUR This zucchini is excellent. You must tell me how to prepare it some time. I've never even thought of preparing zucchini.

CATHERINE I have a few more ingredients to get and then I'll tell sis you're here. She'll be very excited. *(She exits)*

FLEUR Now, I want you to know, Anna, that we're all with you. We all want you to get better and rest and come back to us soon. We all talk about how much we miss you at the lunch table. You always

had a funny story, and so much spirit; we just don't
know what to talk about any more. *(She watches* ANNA
chewing) You just go right on eating. I thought you'd
be finished with supper by now. The zucchini is
really excellent. *(She puts a little more on her own plate)*
Bob and I got in such a fight over whether we should
have bought you a religious article or not. I told him
in times like these you'd appreciate something of
faith and he said I was crazy. He doesn't think anyone believes in religion any more. Of course, I see
the fallout of religious conviction in the children
during my guidance sessions with them. It isn't that
they don't *believe* in religion; children don't even
think about it any more. I thought you'd like a nice
gold cross with a chain, but Bob said even if you
were religious you'd have plenty of them, and I told
him I never saw you wear one at school.

ANNA   I don't wear crosses.

FLEUR   That's just what I told Bob. Since I didn't see
you wearing any crosses I was fairly sure that you
wouldn't appreciate a faith gift, which is why we
got you what we finally did. It's so difficult to believe
in anything, although I did a paper on this called "Is
God Dead?" For a Problems in Modern Living
course I took with Dr. Nobinsky, whose main problem at the time was senility—he's dead now—and I
called my study "Is God Dead?" Now, the title

wasn't very original but I felt I had translated the complex reasons why nobody believes in religion any more. To put it in a nutshell, the reason everyone is so schizophrenic and paranoic today is because man is finally being able to do what he previously thought only a God could do. So because scientific miracles are all around us, we're searching for more brilliant images to worship. (FLEUR *takes more zucchini*) You don't believe in religion at all?

ANNA   Not since Mr. Fisher's puppy.
(CATHERINE *enters and begins noisily dicing a banana on a cutting board*)

FLEUR   Mr. Fisher's puppy?

ANNA   Oh, yes. You know Mr. Fisher, that nice old man with the gas station on Bay Street? The Mobil station.

FLEUR   I don't use Mobil. I've been going to the Gulf at the corner of Clove and Victory. They're giving mugs.

ANNA   Anyway, Mr. Fisher with the Mobil station had a puppy two years ago and he doesn't have a puppy any more.
(CATHERINE *goes into the kitchen*)

FLEUR   I wonder what could be keeping Bob.

ANNA   I was teaching at Jefferson, which was in the

other direction from where Catherine was, so I had to depend upon this teacher Faith Farber, a crippled teacher whose father is a Christian Scientist, which is the reason Faith Farber is a cripple—well, Faith Farber was driving me to school, which used to drive me crazy watching her twisted leg search for the gas pedal.

FLEUR Oh, my. I should think it would, you poor thing.

ANNA I had to watch the road closely because her reflexes are so bad sometimes she used to put on the windshield wipers instead of the brakes . . .

FLEUR Oh, that could be dangerous . . .

ANNA And we were driving by Mr. Fisher's Mobil gas station when this little puppy comes running right out in front of the car, but we stopped in time.

FLEUR Thank God.

ANNA And there's this cute little puppy looking at me sitting in Faith Farber's suicide seat, and he's wagging his tail a mile a minute and looking so grateful . . .

FLEUR (Nervously eating zucchini) That is cute . . .

ANNA I'm not finished yet! Because then the puppy decides to go back the way he came, which is right in front of me in the death seat, when this big trailer truck comes zipping along right there, right out my window, and I yelled out, "NO, PUPPY! NO, PUPPY!" And the truck driver sees what's going on and he jams on his brakes, but the front wheels come to a stop right on the back half of this little puppy, squirting his guts across the road. (FLEUR *begins to choke*) I let out a scream and the little puppy is still alive, his legs rammed out toward me, his eyes looking right at me—and he's saying, "Ehhhhhhhh! ehhhhhhhh!" And then the truck moves ahead and the back wheels go right over the puppy's head and paws and the rest of it, and there's only this little wet spot on the road. And Mr. Fisher, old, poor Mr. Fisher, whose wife had died the year before—old Mr. Fisher comes running out of his Mobil service station and he took one look and passed out, banging his head on the concrete. *(A pause)* That was the last day I wore crosses.

FLEUR Oh, my—yes. I need water. Excuse me.
(She rushes to the table for a glass of water. She sets the zucchini down, and pours herself a glass of water from a pitcher on the desk. The door buzzer rings)

ANNA Come on in!
(BOB enters. He is wearing a business suit; he moves in a self-assured manner)

FLEUR   Bob, what took you so long?

ANNA   Do you have my present?

BOB *(Braying)*   What do you mean what took me so long? Don't you remember where we had to park this afternoon? *(To* ANNA*)* Sure, I got your present.

ANNA   *(Grabbing it from him and going back to her seat)* This box is pretty small for ten dollars.

CATHERINE *(Entering)*   Oh, Bob.

BOB   Hi-ya, Catherine, how the hell are you?

CATHERINE   We were just going to have dessert. Shall I make enough for you?

FLEUR   Just a nibble for me.

ANNA   You'll have to put four kiwis in it then.

CATHERINE   Yes, Anna. Four kiwis.

BOB *(Looking at the vegetables)*   I'll just fix myself a drink.
        (He helps himself)

FLEUR *(To* ANNA*)*   We got them at Prussacks. I really hope you like them.

BOB   I was doubled-parked for ten minutes on Richmond Avenue while she was running around like a chicken with her head cut off. And if they think I'm paying thirty-five dollars for that lousy garage downstairs, they're crazy.

(ANNA *has finished opening her package, and she slowly lifts out a pair of gloves*)

FLEUR I thought something warm . . .

ANNA *(Screaming as she throws the gloves and box across the room)* I don't want them! Get them out of here!

FLEUR Pardon me?

ANNA Get them out of here.

CEIL *(Entering)* The gloves are leather and they're fur-lined. *(She picks them up)* My sister doesn't want anything killed.

CATHERINE Fleur and Bob, I want you to meet my dear sister, Ceil Adams. Ceil, darling, this is Fleur and Bob Stein.

CEIL Hello. I'm sorry . . . *(She goes to pick up the gloves and replace them in their box)* Anna doesn't care for fur apparel.

ANNA I hate fur.

BOB My mother hated fur, too. She said it was a waste of money. You can get a good pair of wool gloves for half that, and they'd be just as good.

FLEUR   Of course. *(She digs in her handbag)* I've got the receipt, and you can just go back down and get something you *would* like.

BOB   I told her to get a gift certificate, but no! She had to go running around like a chicken with its head cut off.

FLEUR   Bob, I wish you wouldn't use that expression.

BOB   But it's true; you run around like a chicken with its head cut off.

FLEUR   I was going to get flowers . . .

CEIL   It was a very kind gesture, Mrs. Stein. We appreciate it.

FLEUR   Thank you. Mrs. Adams, I'm so very glad to meet you. I had wanted to meet you for months when I found out Catherine was your sister and we lived in the very same apartment building. I think you're one of the most amazing Board of Education superintendents this city has ever had. Whenever they speak of you down at school it's with supreme admiration, and when Mrs. Pentrano told me you were here tonight, I just so much wanted to see you. Of course, I did want to deliver Anna's present on behalf of the Social Committee—she was a magnificent science teacher, she really is—and Catherine is the finest AA I've worked under.

BOB Fleur, your hypertension is showing.

FLEUR I wish you wouldn't use that word, Bob. I really do wish you wouldn't.

CEIL I didn't get your first name, Mrs. Stein.

FLEUR It's Fleur. That's French for flower. Think of snow *flur*-ries. That's the best way to remember it. I'm in Child Guidance, down there with Anna and Catherine—she truly is just a marvelous AA, really. I'm not a licensed guidance teacher; I'm an *acting* guidance teacher—

BOB But the only difference between being an acting guidance teacher and a licensed guidance teacher is she doesn't get the salary she deserves.

FLEUR Bob, please don't talk like that. It's embarrassing.

BOB Look, I'm on the outside of that kooky profession and I've got a right to express my opinion.

FLEUR (*To* CEIL) He's in glass. In Pawling Glass, the medium-priced glass you probably heard of; not too cheap, not too expensive.

BOB I've got the Virgin Islands and I make a good buck. I get a little fishing in, too.

FLEUR   He certainly does. He's hardly ever home. Actually, Mrs. Adams, you and I should have met a long time ago, since Bob knew your husband at school—they both were at Wagner College together —a special course, didn't you say, Bob?

BOB   That's what I said. Some weird course in real estate, which I never went into.

FLEUR   Well, I was going out with Bob at that time. We were a late marriage, too, and I think it's a credit to schoolteachers that we don't marry right off the bat—shows we learn something from all those psych courses. Anyway, Bob was commuting all the way to Newark to date me, and since he was such friends with your husband—Edward—I mean, in the same course and all, wouldn't it seem as if we might have double-dated at least? Bob and me and you and Edward?

BOB   Fleur, I told you I hardly knew Edward Adams. We were in this one course together, and we never said one word to each other. I didn't even sit near him.

FLEUR   But still we might have double-dated. The possibility exists.

ANNA   Edward wasn't dating Ceil at that time, so the possibility doesn't exist.

FLEUR Bob, you said Edward Adams was going out with the Reardon sister when he was in that course with you.

CATHERINE *(Goes out quickly, holding back tears)* Anna, if you want this dessert, come out to the kitchen and help me cut up some of this fruit. It's making too much of a mess in here.

ANNA *(To* FLEUR*)* Don't finish off the zucchini while I'm gone.
(She follows CATHERINE *into the kitchen)*

CEIL *(After silence has fallen)* Edward was friends with my sister first—and then he married me.

FLEUR Oh!

BOB Kept him in the family anyway. *(He laughs, adding to the embarrassment, and nervously opens the Fanny Farmer candy box which is next to him. His face squirms in disbelief)* Dear, I think we'd better get going.

FLEUR We have plenty of time. I deliberately allowed time, Bob, and you know that very well. *(To* CEIL*)* Bob said only the nicest things about Edward Adams, didn't you, Bob? He was very creative, I understand. Artistic. What did he finally go into?

CEIL He's with an oil company. He likes it very much.

FLEUR   One of the more creative departments? Advertising? Art?

CEIL   He's in quality control.

BOB   That's a surprise. Everybody used to think he'd end up in some arty-darty thing.

FLEUR   I'm sure his work *is* creative, Bob. And you wouldn't really know if it was or not, since you're all business.

BOB   There's nothing wrong with being able to make a buck in business, is there?

CEIL   Your job must be interesting, Mr. Stein. The Virgin Islands are very lovely.

BOB   I make half my money on being sensible. If there was anything artistic in me, I would have been killed off years ago.

FLEUR   I'm sure being in oil and being in glass are two different things.

BOB   I wish you'd stop saying I'm "*in* glass"! I am not "*in* glass."
      (ANNA *enters with an egg and other ingredients*)

CEIL   It was very nice meeting you. I assume you're going somewhere this evening . . .

ANNA   Our guests are staying for dessert, *Ceil.*
(*She breaks the raw egg into the blender*)

FLEUR   If we leave in fifteen minutes or so, we'll make
it to the theater in plenty of time.

BOB   We're going to an ice show, not "the theater."

FLEUR   I believe it takes place in a theater, Bob. I
prefer the mental provocation of Broadway dramas,
but my husband falls asleep.

BOB   I'm in the room, so you could refer to me as *Bob*
and everyone will know who you mean.
(ANNA *goes back into the kitchen*)

FLEUR   As I wanted to say, Mrs. Adams, I'm in the
middle of the guidance exam right now. I had failed
it twice before, not the written part—I always pass
the written part—but it's the interview that I have
trouble with. Those three administrators just sitting
across the room firing questions at me—that's the
part I fail.

CEIL   The oral?

FLEUR   Yes, the oral. The written is fine—really excellent—but the oral, I just always fail the oral.

BOB   I'm sure Mrs. Adams don't give a damn about
your oral problems or anything to do with that
school after hours. That's one thing I put a stop to

in our apartment—no school talk. There's something queer about teachers the way they can't turn it off even in bed.

(ANNA *enters with a handful of fruit for the blender*)

FLEUR   Bob, you *are* embarrassing me.

BOB   Well, it's true. What the hell good are all those goddam paid vacation days you get when you can't even turn it off on a tour of Europe?

FLEUR   Some people might call it dedication, dear.

BOB   (*To* CEIL)   Do you know what my wife had the nerve to say to me . . . ?

ANNA   Her name is *Fleur*.

BOB   What?

ANNA   Her name is *Fleur*. You could just say *Fleur* and since she's in the room we'd all know who you were talking about.

BOB   Do you know what Fleur had the nerve to say to me when we were 12,673 feet up in a cable car over the Alps?

FLEUR   Bob, now you're telling tales yourself out of school.

BOB   . . . 12,673 feet high in the air, three European panoramic countries laying out in front of us—three thousand bucks invested to drag our butts over to this vista of beauty—and she leans over and whispers in my ear *(Mimicking his wife's voice):* "Do you see the little girl in the cable car ahead of us? . . . "

FLEUR   Bob, there's no need for you to . . .

BOB   "Did you see the little girl in the cable car ahead of us because . . . because she looks just like Dorothy Pewkar, the girl I had programmed out of Political Science." The Pewkar girl. Dorothy Pewkar! I mean, that girl—whoever the hell she may be—has got a lot more problems than whether Fleur Stein programmed her out of Political Science, not the least of which is having a name like Dorothy Pewkar. Do you mind if I use your bathroom?

ANNA   It's right through there.

FLEUR   You don't have to use the bathroom, Bob.

BOB   Fleur, what the hell do you mean I don't have to use the bathroom? You have methodically and expertly taken control of all choice and behavior in my life except my bladder and bowels.

FLEUR   *(Fumbling in her purse)*   Look, here's the key to our apartment. Go back upstairs and use our bathroom.

BOB   I have a key to my own apartment, dear. You may have forgotten but I live there, too—and I pass in and out of the door under my own control. I swear to God you're *hyper* tonight.

ANNA Oh, go ahead and use our bathroom.

FLEUR Don't mess up the towels.

BOB What the hell did you think I was going to do? Hurl them off the walls?
(He exits down the hallway to the bathroom)

FLEUR He has such faulty manners sometimes.

CEIL He's probably just anxious to get started—to the theater.

FLEUR He has some kind of problem left over from his mother.

ANNA The one that hates furs?

FLEUR Do you know he never uses the bathroom in our apartment? We've been married almost nine years and he's never used it. I suspect he uses the one at his office. (ANNA *returns to the kitchen*) Mrs. Adams, I want to tell you I am very sorry about this whole affair. That's why I really stopped by tonight. You must feel absolutely dreadful, your own sister being accused of doing something sexual with a young adult, but there is no disgrace to it, no disgrace. Every time we discuss it at school there is no disgrace, and you mustn't feel there is. The boy's parents—the McCloud mother and father—were up to school, and the principal and I handled them. They were furious when they first came in, and the mother began to scream at me, and I told her I was only a guidance teacher and that her behavior was quite out of line. Anyway, I think I've talked them out of suing. (ANNA *enters from the kitchen, mildly sensing the tension in the room, and makes final preparations at the blender.* FLEUR *shifts to a stage whisper*) So instead of that *party* coming down to school, I told them I'd visit them at their home for our next meeting; it'd be less awkward, although it means extra work for me, but I don't mind.

CEIL   I don't think now is the right time to go into this, Mrs. Stein. It'd be better if you called me at my office on Monday.

FLEUR   I'll be happy to, Mrs. Adams. I just wanted you to know I was doing everything I can on the matter.

CEIL   Did you understand me, Mrs. Stein?

FLEUR   Oh, yes, Mrs. Adams, Yes, indeed.

CATHERINE   *(Reentering from the kitchen)*   Where's Bob?

ANNA   He's in the john. He doesn't use the john in his own apartment.

CATHERINE Why not?

FLEUR That's what I was telling Anna before. There's
something wrong with all of us, and we're really not
to blame for it. The world just got too complex and
all our idols came crashing down—just like what
happened to the Egyptians and the Romans—I was
telling Anna I did a paper on it, showing how the
collapse of our modern world is coming about because we've finally reached a point of scientific con-
sciousness which overreaches our former religious
goals. *(Pause of embarrassment)* You know, I used to
think I failed the orals because the interviewers
were anti-Semitic, but I checked up on them and
they were all Jewish. (BOB *enters puffing on a cigarette*)
Did you light that cigarette up in their bathroom?

BOB No, I saw smoke coming out of the hot-water
faucet and when I looked, this Kent mentholated
filter-tip was rammed up in it.

FLEUR I just don't know why men insist on lighting
up cigarettes when they go into a bathroom. My
father did the same thing, and I found it revolting.
(FLEUR *takes a big mouthful of zucchini*)

ANNA Did you know that eating the right combina-
tion of vegetables makes your feces odorless?
(FLEUR *gags, and* CATHERINE *turns on the blender.
Finally, she shuts it off*)

CATHERINE *(Peering into the blender)* I think we've got the right combination.
(She starts to serve it)

FLEUR Excuse me, but I have to use the bathroom.
(She runs from the room)

BOB *(Yelling after her)* Don't mess up the towels! *(He laughs)* She's so sick it isn't funny. I mean, the Board of Ed is batty, but at least they know enough not to give a bewildered schizo a license. Some nights I lay awake trying to picture what on earth she guides down there.

CEIL Mr. Stein, you may not realize it but it takes many years of experience and maturing to be a guidance teacher.

BOB If she matures much more she's going to be dead! I think they don't give her a regular license 'cause they know she doesn't know what the hell she's doing.

ANNA *(Handing BOB his dessert)* Just try a little. It's good for you.

BOB *(Still focused on CEIL)* They have two other guidance teachers down at that school, and they got their licenses and everything. The others get normal maladjusted bastards, but they give Fleur the teenage insane. *(He takes a sip of his dessert, and opens his mouth as though it's on fire)* What the hell is this?

ANNA You don't like it?

BOB It's rotten! What're you drinking it for?

ANNA I had rabies, and the doctors want me to build up my system.

BOB You had rabies? Are you nuts?

CEIL Mr. Stein, if you don't mind. When Fleur comes back I think you'd better leave . . .

BOB Look, Anna . . . Catherine, we're sort of friends. I'm not the kind of big phony that can just stand here, making believe I don't know what's going on. *(To ANNA)* I frankly was shocked when Fleur told me what you did.

CEIL We're not going to discuss the matter, Mr. Stein, and I'm a little shocked your wife was so unprofessional as to discuss it with you.

BOB That's probably the reason Anna did what she did—because you never felt like discussing. But I'm not no phony. When you pretend things don't exist —that they never happened—it gets worse in the mind, don't it, Anna? There was a teacher who did something like what Anna did when I went to Davidson High. Even when I was thirteen—I was thirteen—and I knew what was wrong with her. She even had a sick mother and do you know where she kept her mother's bed? Right in the middle of the living room. It's no good when all you've got is women around.

CATHERINE Bob, would you be courteous enough to shut your big goddam mouth?

BOB Look, Catherine, I didn't mean to put this on a personal level. What's done is done. I think the two of you could use a little male influence, that's all I'm saying—and then maybe Anna wouldn't have gotten so sick.

CEIL Anna will be seeing the best doctors, Mr. Stein . . .

BOB Since when are psychiatrists the best doctors? Every one I ever knew was a pervert. Her sister lives next door to one in Perth Amboy who chokes milk bottles and beats his lettuce. All Anna's got to do is get out a little. You've got to get out and meet some men.

FLEUR (*Entering*) It's a very cheerful bathroom. Those angelfish decals . . .

BOB (*Continuing to* ANNA) You know how dumb men are. You just got to go where they are. Jesus Christ,

I mean even a neighborhood bar, or get the hell out of teaching and work in advertising or something.

FLEUR   Bob, Mrs. Adams said . . .

BOB (*To* FLEUR)   Shut up. (*To* ANNA) Sure, there's a lot of pretty boys in that, but if you're just around the same guys long enough, sooner or later one of 'em will notice you and think he loves you and before you know it you'll be married.

FLEUR   Mrs. Adams doesn't want this matter mentioned.

BOB (*To* ANNA)   When was the last time you ever went out anywhere, except to some free teachers' luncheon at the French Embassy or some crap like that?

CATHERINE   Bob, get your ass out of here.

FLEUR (*Putting her fur on*)   We'd better be going, Bob. You know how you like the overture.

BOB (*To* ANNA)   Even an ice show? Don't you ever go out and have fun? How the hell are you going to meet any men, sitting around here?

FLEUR (*Going to* BOB, *who is hovering behind* ANNA)   Bob, let's get out of here . . .

BOB (*To* ANNA)   Why the hell don't you come along with Fleur and me tonight? Go throw a dress on, and I'll get an extra ticket and we'll go to some cocktail lounge afterward, and I'll get a guy for you. Just someone to talk to. The four of us. Get into the swing of things.

CATHERINE   She's not going anywhere. You're the one that's going . . .

FLEUR   Bob, *really* . . .

BOB   I'll make Fleur lend you her fur . . .
(*He takes the stole off* FLEUR)

FLEUR   Bob, she doesn't . . .

BOB   You're not half bad-looking, Anna, no kidding. You'll look snazzy as hell . . .

FLEUR   Bob . . . the fur gloves . . . She doesn't care for fur . . .

BOB   (*Stretching the stole out behind* ANNA *like the wings of a condor*)   You'll knock 'em dead!
(*He drops the stole around* ANNA*'s shoulders.* ANNA *shivers from the fur, then throws the stole to the floor and kicks it violently several times*)

FLEUR   (*Finally*)   She told you she didn't like fur, Bob.

CATHERINE   Would anyone like a little more kiwi frappe?

BOB *(Dumbfounded)* My mother never hated fur that much.

CEIL Anna is a vegetarian, Mr. Stein. She doesn't like animals being killed.

BOB *(His amazement giving way to fury)* You've got one hell of a nerve kicking my wife's fur around like that. ONE HELL OF A NERVE!

FLEUR Bob, Mrs. Adams told you she's a vegetarian . . .

ANNA *(Indicating FLEUR)* If she wants to run around with animal corpses hanging all over her, that's her business. All those beautiful tiny animals raised in little cages that had to get gassed and have the skin ripped off their backs so some loud-mouth, hyper slob can squat on her big fat ass at an ice show.
(She gets seconds on the dessert)

FLEUR She *told* you she hated furs, Bob . . .

BOB So you're a vegetarian, eh?

FLEUR Mrs. Adams said she was, Bob . . .

BOB A vegetarian, eh? Well, you're demented. You're just one more of those fanatics that pick out one ittsie thing and march around making believe you're not trying to cover up some sick, twisted problem you've got.

FLEUR Bob!

BOB What do you think you're wearing on your feet? Those slippers. They're leather, you stupid little fool! You're as inconsistent as the rest of those insane fanatics.

CATHERINE Don't call my sister a stupid little fool, you schmuck.

ANNA (*Holding one foot up in the air*) They're Leatherette! You dummy! Leatherette! (*She roars at him*) Ha!

CEIL Anna, that's enough . . .

BOB Oh, yeah? How about the top of this cigarette box? That's leather. Leather all over it. I'll bet you didn't notice that. (ANNA *looks at the cigarette box and throws it against the door*) Inconsistent, that's what you are. Just like all those revolutionaries. You've got animal skins and corpses all over this place, honey, and you'd better learn to live with 'em. And that's one hell of a box of Fanny Farmer candy you've got over there!

CATHERINE Bob, your mentality isn't in glass, it's in horseshit.

FLEUR Let's go, Bob. We're going to be late as it is.

BOB Inconsistency! You can't even see it, can you? I heard how you went around picking up all those goddam cats in Italy. Picking up all those animals and giving 'em a little love; worrying about those little pussy cats starving to death; just hugging and petting 'em and rubbing 'em . . . Jesus Christ, no wonder you're afraid of rabies. That vegatarian crap is only a cover-up for your real problem. You've cut out a whole part of living. You might just as well have sliced off a piece of your body.

FLEUR Bob, Mrs. Adams is my supervisor and you're embarrassing me. I'm very embarrassed.

BOB Oh, embarrass later. She knows what you're here for. (*To* ANNA) You could kick that fur all the way down to Forty-second Street, and everybody's still going to know you're a cripple. You and Catherine. Catherine, I never knew you had such a repulsive mouth.
     (There is a terrible silence)

CATHERINE *(Sipping her drink; then sweetly)* Anna? Isn't there something in the album you'd like to show Mr. Stein?
     (ANNA *remembers the gun; starts for the album*)

Curtain

ACT THREE

The curtain rises as ANNA *continues her cross toward the album containing the gun.*

BOB   If you knew how many nights Fleur and I sat up there in our apartment talking about you two, you'd realize we're the best friends you've got in the world. I mean it, Catherine.

CATHERINE   Anna has something to show you in our album, Bob.

ANNA   Yes, Bob. Come here.

BOB   *(Staying where he is)*   We saw this whole thing coming, Fleur and me. Only, I thought it was going to be you first, Catherine.

CATHERINE   Then it's only the juxtaposition that's disturbed you . . .

BOB   *(Moving toward* ANNA, *who is holding the gun and album)*   Ceil's the one that had the guts to get away from Mama. She was the biggest lulu, that mother of yours.

ANNA   Look at this, Mr. Stein.

BOB   The best thing that ever happened to the three of you was when she kicked the bucket.
(ANNA *lifts the gun out of the album and fires it point-blank at* BOB)

FLEUR   Oh, my God!

BOB   (*Choking from the shock, grabbing the gun and seeing it was a blank*) You crazy goddam fool. You could have burned my eyes. (*To* CATHERINE) And you put her up to it. You two are birds of a feather, you are. Two loony birds.

FLEUR   Bob . . . it was a jest. I'm sure it was just a jest.

BOB   (*Recovered from the choking, exploding at* ANNA) Who the hell do you think you are firing that thing at me, you little sick bitch? You've got problems, girl, real problems.

ANNA   (*Furiously*)   I have *what*?

BOB   Problems. You got real problems.

ANNA   I have problems, eh?

BOB   That's what I said. You don't like to hear that? *Problems.* You got big problems.

ANNA You have a little problem, too, don't you, Mr. Stein? I'm very interested in your problem—the problem about why you never use the bathroom in your own house? Your wife was telling us how you never use your own bathroom—it's been nine years, didn't you say, Fleur?—nine years of not using the bathroom in your own house, so we were wondering if *you* had a little problem?

BOB *(Exasperated, he hurries to his coat, puts it on, and then grabs* FLEUR*'s handbag)* Give me my goddam ticket. *(He finds the tickets and takes one)* I'm going outside, and I'll wait exactly three minutes, and if you're not out of this nut house by then, I'm leaving without you.

FLEUR I'll be right down.

BOB *(To* ANNA*)* You know, when I first heard what you did down at that school I didn't believe it, but now I do! *(He storms toward the door, opens it, then pauses. Almost trembling, he turns around and faces them)* Do you want to know why I don't use the bathroom in our apartment? Do you really want to know? Well, I'm going to tell you. I don't like using our bathroom because everything in that bathroom my wife steals from the Board of Education. That's why!

FLEUR Bob . . .

BOB You know that attaché case my wife runs around
with, like a chicken with her head cut off? She only
drags it around so every time she goes to the ladies'
room at that school she loads up on paper towels,
soap, and toilet paper.

FLEUR Oh, my God . . .

BOB She also steals the sugar and salt from the teachers' lunchroom—as well as so many paper napkins
she keeps her mother in napkins—she packs that
attaché case up with so much crap sometimes I have
to help her carry the loot out of the goddam car.

FLEUR Bob, do you realize what you're saying?

BOB So, I'll tell you why I don't use the bathroom in
our apartment. I don't use our bathroom because I
don't like drying my hands with brown, stiff paper-
towels, I don't like washing my face with Twenty
Mule Team Borax, I don't like taking a bath in Fels-
Naphtha, and I don't like using toilet tissue that has
a texture like sandpaper to wipe my ass!
(He exits, slamming the door)

FLEUR *(After a long silence)* I don't know what to say.
(A pause) Almost nothing of what he said is true. He
always did have such a good imagination that he
exaggerates and distorts so much that his lies seem

true. I don't know whether he's just jealous of the fact that I make more money than he does. He's only an assistant district manager, and he doesn't work on commissions. Maybe I should have quit my job when we married—maybe it would have made him work harder. He's hardly ever home . . . *(She is on the verge of crying)* Mrs. Adams, it's been a pleasure meeting you . . . *(She pauses; begins to find strength)* I really did want you to know I was doing everything I could with the McCloud parents. They seem to trust me and I think I can stop them from suing. I know I could, if you'd agree to put Anna away . . . for treatment. They're insisting on that . . .

CATHERINE Beat it, Fleur!

FLEUR *(Getting stronger)* I'm working extra hard on the case. I even agreed to those extra sessions at their home. I'll keep it out of the school. I haven't told anyone except Bob. No one down there knows the details. And I just thought, Mrs. Adams, if you could remember me down at the Board . . . about my license . . . *(Almost demanding)* It would be wonderful of you, Mrs. Adams. Very wonderful.
  (CATHERINE *turns on the blender.* FLEUR *exits, and* CATHERINE *halts the blender)*

CEIL Anna, go to your room and lie down.

ANNA Go to your own goddam room!

CEIL   Tell her to leave us alone.

CATHERINE   Now, sis, it is a bit tardy for disciplinary procedures.

CEIL   Catherine . . .

ANNA   Oh, Ceil . . . Can't you remember all the fun when we were just getting started as teachers? How we'd all come running home at three o'clock, and Mama'd have the water boiling and some kind of pie made with Flako pie-crust mix? And Mama'd be dying to know what happened in school all day, and we'd be dying to tell her—and we'd sit around this same table and almost pass out laughing? We'd tell Mama what was going on in the schools, and she wouldn't believe it. She'd say the whole world was going crazy. Remember when I told her about little Gracie Ratinski, that nutty kid with bugs in her hair at Jefferson who used to come into the cafeteria and sing her lunch order out at the top of her lungs? "Give me a peanut butter sandwich, tra la. Give me a peanut butter sandwich, tra la." Don't you remember that? Don't you?

CATHERINE   I remember. I remember, all right. And remember how much Mama laughed when I told her about Rose Anadale, the principal at P.S. 26 who kept the parakeet in her office . . .

ANNA She used to talk about it on the P.A. system every morning after *The Star-Spangled Banner* . . .

CATHERINE She'd announce to the whole school, remember: "Good morning, children . . . Good morning, children . . . Little Polly and I hope you have a wonderful day."

ANNA And remember how Mama laughed when I told her about one of my underprivileged parents calling in to say her underprivileged kid wouldn't be able to take the General Science midterm because she had to go to the church rectum? (CATHERINE *and* ANNA *howl, but it is obvious that* CATHERINE *is watching the effect on* CEIL) Don't you miss telling Mama those stories? Don't you miss it?

CEIL Tell her to leave us alone.

CATHERINE Look, Ceil, it's late—you probably have to get up early tomorrow and appoint a committee to study the salient factors of some nonsense or other . . .

CEIL If that's the way you want it . . . *(A pause)* I've made arrangements . . .

CATHERINE You don't say. They are floral, aren't they?

CEIL She's going to a hospital.

CATHERINE No kidding. Far away? Tudor or Swiss? Mountains and view of lake? No, don't tell me the preponderating feature. It's state-supported.

CEIL All you have to do is get her packed.

ANNA She's the one that needs a rest, Catherine. She's very tired. Very tired and very sick.

CEIL *(Taking papers out of her brief case)* You have to look at these, Catherine.

CATHERINE *(Slamming a serving tray down on the buffet with a resounding noise)* Don't tell me what I have to do.
   (There is long silence; finally)

ANNA Ceil, didn't you ever love us? Mama? Any of us?

CEIL Our lives are not around this table any more.

ANNA Oh—I must have forgotten. This is all dead now, isn't it? Silent. The voices gone. Even the whispering forgotten: "Straighten up . . . careful your slip isn't showing . . . skirt down . . . knees close together. Be careful if someone sits next to you—or across the way. Beware of your eyes . . . He mustn't think you're looking at him. Even when you're . . . bleeding, he'll know. He'll try to find a way . . . to force you apart . . . to cut into you . . ." And the sounds—you must have forgotten the sounds in the dark of our rooms . . . the quieting of the wounds by which we could be tracked. Tell me what you and Edward do. Does he actually manage to get on top and ride you like some blubbery old nag?

(ANNA *rips the papers out of* CEIL *'s hands. Furiously,* CEIL *grabs the Fanny Farmer box and smears the chopped meat into* ANNA *'s face.* ANNA *falls to her knees, senses the meat, and screams as though bathed in spiders. She runs out of the room, down the hallway.* CATHERINE *tries to go after* ANNA)

CEIL   She can wash herself.

(CEIL *physically stops* CATHERINE *from passing*)

CATHERINE   Get out of my way!

CEIL   How the hell much longer did you think you could go on keeping her here?

CATHERINE   As long as I want, that's how long.

CEIL   Why? So you won't be alone? After all the filth and wisecracks are scraped off is that what's underneath?

CATHERINE   *(Ringing the buffet bell)* School's over. Everybody's dismissed.

(CEIL *yanks the bell out of* CATHERINE *'s hand*)

CEIL   Don't you think I need anything?

CATHERINE   I thought you always took everything you needed.

CEIL   Anything I did you made me do after the years of gnawing at me—you and her and Mama. The whole pack of you. For what? What was it you hated so much?

CATHERINE *(Exploding)*   I'll tell you what and I'll tell you when! You see, there was this big hole in the ground, with you on one side of it and me on the other—and we were watching them stick a coffin in the ground. But as it was going down I had to shut my eyes because I'll tell you all I could see: I saw you with a lawyer making sure the few bucks of a croaking old lady were transferred to your name. And I was admiring a casket you picked out that wouldn't waste a second getting her corpse back to ashes. And I remembered when that imperfect gasping woman was dying how you made certain you didn't have to touch a penny in your bank account.

CEIL   That's not what you hated me for *all* your life! Anything you didn't like you could have done differently. Anything! You're not going to blame me for that or anything about your sick little life. You didn't have to follow me—let me do everything. I didn't bend anybody's arm. You could have lived your own lives, you know. You didn't have to feed on me all the time!

CATHERINE   Get out of here.

CEIL   What is it deep down in your gut you so detest about me? That I haven't gone mad or become an obscene nasty witness? That's what you are, Catherine.

CATHERINE   You know, Ceil—the way you said that— I mean, you're louder and crueller—but there's a part of you that's just like Mama. I think that's the part of you I've always despised.
> (CATHERINE *turns away.* CEIL *gets her coat from the closet and gathers up the papers, the gun and the album*)

CEIL   I'll call you in the morning.

CATHERINE *(Pouring a drink)* Not in the morning, if you don't mind. You see, Miss Reardon drinks a little and she'll be sleeping off a colossal load.

CEIL *(Throwing the album, gloves and papers to the floor)* Here! Here's everything. I'm not going to let you pin the rap on me or Mama or anybody any more. Now it's up to you. For once in your life, you pick up the pieces however the hell you want. But no matter what you do, let me tell you this: You're not going to drag me down. Not at this stage of the game, my sweet sisters. Not at this stage of the game.

(CEIL *exits, leaving* CATHERINE *sitting at the desk.* ANNA *enters*)

ANNA You're worse than all of them. You never do anything to stop the destruction.

CATHERINE I got rid of her. What else do you want from me?

ANNA You're godless and you're killing all of us. Everything.

CATHERINE Look, I'm warning you. I'm going shopping tomorrow and I'm buying roast beef, frankfurters, liverwurst, knockwurst, and two pounds of Virginia ham. It may sound primitive but it sure as hell's going to be delicious. (ANNA *heads to lock the door*) Don't lock the door!

(ANNA *stops, slowly moves back to her place at the table*)

ANNA Catherine—sometimes . . . sometimes I see my reflection in a window . . . or look down at my hand resting in my lap, and I see her. Mama. She's inside of me. She frightens me, Catherine. She makes me afraid. I look out the window . . . the telephone poles in the street . . . she makes me see them as dead crucifixes. I'm losing my mind. I can't stop myself. She's at my throat now. Catherine, she's strangling me. Help me. Oh, God, help me . . .

(She puts her head on the table)

CATHERINE *(Pauses, rises, turns off the floor lamp, goes to the hall and turns off the foyer light)* Everyone's going crazy, Anna, do you know that? The dentist—I went to the new dentist down the street—I went three weeks ago for my first appointment, and then last week, and then yesterday. He wears three wigs, Anna. On the first visit he was wearing a crew-cut wig. Last week he had a medium-length wig. And yesterday he had this fuzzy llama-wool wig and he kept saying, "Dear me, oh, dear me—I've got to get a haircut . . ." And next week I know he'll have the crew-cut job on again.

(She moves to ANNA, gently touches her. ANNA raises her head slowly and the two sisters behold the now empty family table)

ANNA Catherine—what world were we waiting for?

Curtain

About the Author

PAUL ZINDEL is a major new talent in the American theater. He has been awarded the Pulitzer Prize in Drama for *The Effect of Gamma Rays on Man-in-the-Moon Marigolds*, which is still successfully running off-Broadway and is to be made into a motion picture. In addition, the play won both an Obie Award and the New York Drama Critics' Circle Award for Best American Play. Mr. Zindel's other honors include a Drama Desk Award and the Variety Poll of Critics Award as the outstanding new playwright of the 1970–1971 season.

A native of Staten Island, Mr. Zindel was a chemistry teacher in the public high schools there for ten years. His novels for young adults, *The Pigman, My Darling, My Hamburger* and *I Never Loved Your Mind*, were selected as Outstanding Children's Books of the Year by *The New York Times*. An original television play, *Let Me Hear You Whisper*, was produced by NET. *And Miss Reardon Drinks a Little* is Paul Zindel's first Broadway play. Mr. Zindel is now at work on another drama, a musical and a screenplay.